I0500593

Typed Resource Definitions

Fire and Hazardous Materials Resources

FEMA 508-4

July 2005

Background   The National Mutual Aid and Resource Management Initiative supports the National Incident Management System (NIMS) by establishing a comprehensive, integrated national mutual aid and resource management system that provides the basis to type, order, and track all (Federal, State, and local) response assets.

Resource   For ease of ordering and tracking, response assets need to be categorized via
Typing   resource typing. Resource typing is the categorization and description of resources that are commonly exchanged in disasters via mutual aid, by capacity and/or capability. Through resource typing, disciplines examine resources and identify the capabilities of a resource's components (i.e., personnel, equipment, training). During a disaster, an emergency manager knows what capability a resource needs to have to respond efficiently and effectively. Resource typing definitions will help define resource capabilities for ease of ordering and mobilization during a disaster. As a result of the resource typing process, a resource's capability is readily defined and an emergency manager is able to effectively and efficiently request and receive resources through mutual aid during times of disaster.

Web Site   For more information, you can also refer to the National Mutual Aid and Resource Management Web site located at:

           http://www.fema.gov/nims/mutual_aid.shtm.

Supersedure   This document replaces *Typed Resource Definitions, Fire and Hazardous Materials Resources*, dated May 2005

Changes   Resource table added for Fire Truck - Aerial (Ladder or Platform). Table categories changed as required to comply with NIMS category list.

Table of Contents

RESOURCE:	Area Command Team, Firefighting			
CATEGORY:	Firefighting (ESF #4)	**KIND:**	Team	
MINIMUM CAPABILITIES:				
COMPONENT	**METRIC**	**TYPE I**	**TYPE II**	**TYPE III**	**TYPE IV**	**OTHER**
Personnel	Area Commander (ACDR)	Yes				
Personnel	Asst. Area Commander Planning (ACPC)	Yes				
Personnel	Asst. Area Commander Logistics (ACLC)	Yes				
Personnel	Area Command Aviation Coordinator (ACAC)	Yes				
COMMENTS:	Area Command Team				

COMMENTS continued:

Area Command Team

To become eligible for participating on a National Area Command Team, any person filling a team position as the Area Commander, Assistant Area Commander Planning, Assistant Area Commander Logistics, or Area Command Aviation Coordinator must complete the Area Command (S-620) training course.

Type I Positions:

Area Commander: Prerequisite experience includes satisfactory performance as an Assistant Area Commander Planning or Logistics; satisfactory position performance as an Area Commander on a wildland fire incident. Required Training: Area Command (S-620).

Assistant Area Commander Planning: Prerequisite experience include satisfactory performance as an Incident Commander or General Staff on a National Type I Incident Management Team. Required Training: Area Command (S-620).

Assistant Area Commander Logistics: Prerequisite experience include satisfactory performance as an Incident Commander or General Staff on a National Type I Incident Management Team. Required Training: Area Command (S-620).

Area Command Aviation Coordinator: Prerequisite experience include satisfactory performance as an Air Operations Branch Director on a National Type I Incident Management Team. Required Training: Air Operations Branch Director.

Source: *National Wildfire Coordination Group (NWCG) Publication, National Interagency Incident Management System, Wildland and Prescribed Fire Qualifications System Guide, January 2000 (PMS 310-1, NFES 1414)*.

U.S. Department of Homeland Security
Federal Emergency Management Agency

RESOURCE:	Brush Patrol, Firefighting (Type VI Engine)				
CATEGORY:	Firefighting (ESF #4)		**KIND:**	Equipment	
MINIMUM CAPABILITIES:					
COMPONENT	**METRIC**	**TYPE I**	**TYPE II**	**TYPE III**	**TYPE IV**	**OTHER**
Equipment	Pump					15 GPM
Equipment	Hose					1 inch; 150 feet
Equipment	Tank					75 Gallons
Personnel	Number					1
COMMENTS:	Brush Patrols apply to all vehicles equipped as described.					

FEMA 508-4 Typed Resource Definitions - Fire and Hazardous Materials Resources
07/20/2005

RESOURCE:	Crew Transport (Firefighting Crew)			
CATEGORY:	Firefighting (ESF #4)		**KIND:**	Equipment
MINIMUM CAPABILITIES:	**TYPE I**	**TYPE II**	**TYPE III**	**TYPE IV**	**OTHER**
COMPONENT	**METRIC**				
Personnel	Passengers	30	20	10	
COMMENTS:	Vehicles may be buses, vans, and special crew carrying vehicles (CCV), and may be equipped to carry firefighting tools.				

RESOURCE:	Engine, Fire (Pumper)				
CATEGORY:	Firefighting (ESF #4)		KIND:	Equipment	
MINIMUM CAPABILITIES:					
COMPONENT	METRIC	TYPE I	TYPE II	TYPE III	TYPE IV	OTHER
Equipment	Pump Capacity	1,000 GPM	500 GPM	120 GPM	70 GPM	50 GPM
Equipment	Tank Capacity	400 Gal.	400 Gal.	500 Gal.	750 Gal.	500 Gal.
Equipment	Hose, 2.5 inch	1,200 ft.	1,000 ft.			
Equipment	Hose, 1.5 inch	400 ft.	500 ft.	1,000 ft.	300 ft.	300 ft.
Equipment	Hose, 1 inch	200 ft.	300 ft.	800 ft.	300 ft.	300 ft.
Personnel	Personnel	4	3	3	2	2
COMMENTS:	The engine typing needs to be taken out to Type VI. Compromise between FIRESCOPE and NWCG is to use NWCG Standards for Engines and Crews. NWCG has seven engine types.					

U.S. Department of Homeland Security
Federal Emergency Management Agency

Fire Boat

RESOURCE:					
CATEGORY:	Firefighting (ESF #4)		**KIND:**	Equipment	
MINIMUM CAPABILITIES:		**TYPE I**	**TYPE II**	**TYPE III**	**TYPE IV**	**OTHER**
COMPONENT	**METRIC**					
Equipment	Pump Capacity GPM	5,000	1,000	250		
COMMENTS:	Fire Boats vary in length, draft, and related firefighting equipment.					

Fire Truck - Aerial (Ladder or Platform)

RESOURCE:

CATEGORY: Firefighting, Hazardous Materials Response

KIND: Equipment

MINIMUM CAPABILITIES:

COMPONENT	METRIC	TYPE I	TYPE II	TYPE III	TYPE IV	OTHER
Personnel	Number	4	Same as Type I			
Equipment	Aerial	75 ft	50 ft			
	Elevated Stream	500 GPM	Same as Type I			
	Ground Ladders	115 ft	Same as Type I			

COMMENTS **Note:** Designate "L" for Ladder, or "P" for Platform.

RESOURCE:	Foam Tender, Firefighting				
CATEGORY:	Firefighting (ESF #4); Hazardous Materials Response (ESF #10)		**KIND:**	Equipment	
MINIMUM CAPABILITIES:	**TYPE I**	**TYPE II**	**TYPE III**	**TYPE IV**	**OTHER**
COMPONENT	**METRIC**				
Equipment	Class B Foam	500 gallons	250 gallons		
COMMENTS:	Specify percent of concentrate (1%, 3%, etc.).				

U.S. Department of Homeland Security
Federal Emergency Management Agency

RESOURCE:	Fuel Tender (Gasoline, Diesel, AvGas, aka Gas Tanker)				
CATEGORY:	Transportation (ESF #1); Public Works and Engineering (ESF #3)		KIND:	Equipment	
MINIMUM CAPABILITIES:					
COMPONENT	METRIC	TYPE I	TYPE II	TYPE III	TYPE IV	OTHER
Supply	Fuel	1,000 gal	100 gal			
COMMENTS:	These vehicles vary widely. May be Gasoline, Diesel, Jet Fuel, AvGas, or combinations. Specify: Gas, Diesel, AvGas, etc.					

FEMA 508-4 Typed Resource Definitions - Fire and Hazardous Materials Resources
07/20/2005

RESOURCE:		Hand Crew			
CATEGORY:	Firefighting (ESF #4)		**KIND:** Other - Crew		
MINIMUM CAPABILITIES:					
COMPONENT	METRIC	TYPE I	TYPE II	TYPE III	TYPE IV	OTHER
Personnel	Fireline Capability	Initial attack/can be broken up into squads, fireline construction, complex firing operations (backfire)	Initial attack/can be broken up into squads, fireline construction, firing to include burnout	Initial attack, fireline construction, firing to include burnout	Fireline construction, fireline improvement, mop-up and rehab	
Personnel	Crew Size	18-20	18-20	18-20	18-20	
Personnel	Leadership Qualifications	Permanent Supervision Superintendent: TFLD, ICT4 Asst Supt: STCR, ICT4, 3 Squad Bosses: CRWB(T), ICT5	CRWB and 3 ICT5	CRWB and 3 FFT1	CRWB and 3 FFT1	
Personnel	Experience	80% 1 season or more	60% 1 season or more	40% 1 season or more	20% 1 season or more	
Personnel	Full-Time Organized Crew	Yes	No	No	No	
COMMENTS:	Crews need to be listed as Type I, Type II with Initial Attack Capability, Type II, Type III.				

FEMA

HazMat Entry Team

RESOURCE:							
CATEGORY:	Hazardous Materials Response (ESF #10)			KIND:	Team		
MINIMUM CAPABILITIES:							
COMPONENT	METRIC	TYPE I	TYPE II	TYPE III	TYPE IV	OTHER	
Team	Field Testing	Same as Type II plus: Known or Suspect Weapons of Mass Destruction Chemical/Biological Substances [WMD Chem/Bio]	Same as Type III plus: Unknown Chemicals	Known Chemicals The presumptive testing and identification of chemical substances using a variety of sources to be able to identify associated chemical and physical properties. Sources may include printed and electronic reference resources, safety data sheets, field testing kits, specific chemical testing kits, chemical testing strips, data derived from detection devices, and air-monitoring sources			
Team	Air Monitoring	Same as Type II plus: (WMD Chem/Bio Aerosol Vapor and Gas) Advanced detection and monitoring includes WMD Chem/Bio detection Instruments	Same as Type III plus: The use of advanced detection equipment to detect the presence of known or unknown gases or vapors. Advanced detection and monitoring may incorporate more sophisticated instruments that differentiate between two or more flammable vapors, and may directly identify by name a specific flammable or toxic vapor	(Basic Confined Space Monitoring; Specific Known Gas Monitoring) The use of devices to detect the presence of known gases or vapors. The basics begin with ability to provide standard confined space readings (oxygen deficiency percentage, flammable atmosphere Lower Explosive Limit [LEL], carbon monoxide, and hydrogen sulfide)			

RESOURCE:	HazMat Entry Team				
CATEGORY:	Hazardous Materials Response (ESF #10)		**KIND:** Team		
MINIMUM CAPABILITIES:					
COMPONENT	**METRIC**	**TYPE I**	**TYPE II**	**TYPE III**	**TYPE IV**	**OTHER**
Team	Sampling: Capturing Labeling Evidence Collection	Same as Type II plus: (WMD Chem/Bio) Special resources may be required for air sample collection	Same as Type III plus: (Unknown Industrial Chemicals) Known and unknown industrial chemicals standard evidence collection protocols. Ability to sample liquid and solids	(Known Industrial Chemicals) Known industrial chemicals standard evidence collection protocols required for each include capturing and collection, containerizing and proper labeling, and preparation for transportation and distribution, including standard environmental sampling procedures for lab analysis. Consistent with established chain of custody protocols		
	Radiation Monitoring/ Detection	Same as Type II plus: Identify and establish the exclusion zones after contamination spread (this does include identification of some, but not all, radionuclides). Ability to conduct environmental and personnel survey. Ensure all members of survey teams are equipped with accumulative self-reading instruments (dosimeters)	Same as Type III plus: (Alpha Detection) Basic criteria include detection and survey capabilities for alpha, beta, and gamma	(Beta Detection; Gamma Detection) The ability to accurately interpret readings from the radiation-detection devices and conduct geographical survey search of suspected radiological source or contamination spread. Basic criteria include detection and survey capabilities for beta and gamma		

FEMA

RESOURCE:		HazMat Entry Team				
CATEGORY:		Hazardous Materials Response (ESF #10)		KIND:	Team	
MINIMUM CAPABILITIES:						
COMPONENT	METRIC	TYPE I	TYPE II	TYPE III	TYPE IV	OTHER
Equipment	Protective Clothing: Ensembles	Same as Type II plus: (Weapons of Mass Destruction (WMD) Vapor-Protective CPC; WMD Liquid Splash-Protective CPC) Levels of CPC vapor protection are: Vapor-Protective, Flash Fire Protective option for Vapor-Protective, and Chemical/Biological-Protective option for Vapor-Protective, all of which must be compliant with National Fire Protection Association (NFPA) Standard # 1991, "Standard on Vapor-Protective Ensembles for Hazardous Materials Emergencies" current edition.	Same as Type III plus: (Vapor-Protective CPC; Flash Fire Vapor- Protective CPC) Levels of CPC vapor protection are: Vapor-Protective, and Flash Fire Protective option for Vapor-Protective both of which must be compliant with NFPA Standard # 1991, "Standard on Vapor-Protective Ensembles for Hazardous Materials Emergencies," current edition.	(Liquid Splash-Protective CPC) Chemical Protective Clothing (CPC), which includes complete ensembles (suit, boots, gloves) and may incorporate various configurations (encapsulating, non-encapsulating, jumpsuit, multi-piece) depending upon the level of protection needed. Level of CPC liquid protection is: Liquid Splash-Protective, which must be compliant with NFPA Standard # 1992, "Standard on Liquid Splash-Protective Ensembles and Clothing for Hazardous Materials Emergencies," current edition		
Equipment	Technical Reference	Same as Type II plus: (WMD Chem/Bio)	Same as Type III plus: (Plume Air Modeling; Map Overlays) At a minimum, technical references will have the ability to outsource additional capabilities and have one source for air-modeling capability	(Printed and Electronic) Access to and use of various databases, chemical substance data depositories, and other guidelines and safety data sheets, either in print format, electronic format, stand-alone computer programs, or data available via telecommunications. The interpretation of data collected from electronic		

RESOURCE:	HazMat Entry Team				
CATEGORY:	Hazardous Materials Response (ESF #10)			KIND:	Team
MINIMUM CAPABILITIES:					
COMPONENT	METRIC	TYPE I	TYPE II	TYPE III	TYPE IV	OTHER

COMPONENT	METRIC	TYPE I	TYPE II	TYPE III	TYPE IV	OTHER
				devices and chemical testing procedures		
Equipment	Special Capabilities	Same as Type II plus: (Digital Imaging Documentation Capability)	Same as Type III plus: (Heat Sensing Capability; Light Amplification Capability)	(Gloves and Other Specialized Equipment Based on Local Risk Assessment) Additional resources that augment the capabilities of the team		
Equipment	Intervention	Same as Type II plus: (WMD Chem/Bio Agent Confinement) Advanced capabilities should include ability to intervene and confine incidents involving WMD Chem/Bio substances	Same as Type III plus: (Liquid Leak Intervention; Neutralization; Plugging; Patching; Vapor Leak Intervention) Chemical means such as neutralization and encapsulation of known and unknown chemicals. Mechanical means include specially designed kits for controlling leaks in rail car dome assemblies and pressurized containers, to pneumatic and standard patching systems	(Diking; Damming; Absorption) Employment of mechanical means of intervention and control such as plugging, patching, off-loading, and tank stabilization Environmental means such as absorption, dams, dikes, and booms		
Equipment	Decontamination	Same as Type II plus: (WMD Chem/Bio) Capable of providing decontamination for known and unknown contaminants and WMD Chem/Bio.	Same as Type III plus: (Unknown Contaminants) Capable of providing decontamination for known and unknown contaminants.	(Known Contaminants Based on Local Risk Assessment) Must be self-sufficient to provide decontamination for members of their team. Capable of providing decontamination for known contaminants.		

RESOURCE: HazMat Entry Team

CATEGORY: Hazardous Materials Response (ESF #10) **KIND:** Team

MINIMUM CAPABILITIES:

COMPONENT	METRIC	TYPE I	TYPE II	TYPE III	TYPE IV	OTHER
Equipment	Communications	Same as Type II plus: (Secure Communications)	Same as Type III plus: (Wireless Data)	(In-Suit; Wireless Voice) Personnel utilizing CPC shall be able to communicate appropriately and safely with one another and their team leaders		
Personnel	Staffing	5 Personnel	5 Personnel	5 Personnel		
Personnel	Training	Same as Type II	Same as Type III	All personnel must be trained to the minimum response standards in accordance with the most current editions of NFPA Standard # 471, "Recommended Practice for Responding to Hazardous Materials Incidents," NFPA Standard # 472, "Standard for Professional Competence of Responders to Hazardous Materials Incidents," and NFPA Standard # 473, "Standard for Competencies for EMS Personnel Responding to Hazardous Materials Incidents," as is appropriate for the specific team type		
Personnel	Sustainability	Same as Type II	Same as Type III	Capability to Perform Three (3) Entries in a 24-hour Period		

COMMENTS:

RESOURCE: Helicopters, Firefighting

CATEGORY: Firefighting (ESF #4)

KIND: Aircraft

MINIMUM CAPABILITIES:					
COMPONENT	METRIC	TYPE I	TYPE II	TYPE III	TYPE IV	OTHER
Personnel	Seats, Including Pilot	16	10	5	3	
Equipment	Card Weight Capacity	5,000 lbs	2,500 lbs	1,200 lbs	600 lbs	
Vehicle	Gallons	700	300	100	75	
Supply	Example	Bell 214	Bell 205	Bell 206	Bell 47	

COMMENTS: Firefighting Helicopters may be equipped with rescue, medical, or other equipment.

U.S. Department of Homeland Security
Federal Emergency Management Agency

FEMA

RESOURCE:	Helitanker (firefighting helicopter)				
CATEGORY:	Firefighting (ESF #4)		KIND:	Aircraft	
MINIMUM CAPABILITIES:					
COMPONENT	METRIC	TYPE I	TYPE II	TYPE III	TYPE IV	OTHER
Equipment	Fixed Tank					
Equipment	1100 gal/min					
COMMENTS:	Helitankers are large capacity helicopters (e.g., Sikorsky model) certified by the Air Tanker Board.					

FEMA 508-4 Typed Resource Definitions - Fire and Hazardous Materials Resources
07/20/2005

RESOURCE: Incident Management Team, Firefighting

CATEGORY: Firefighting (ESF #4)   **KIND:** Team

MINIMUM CAPABILITIES:						
COMPONENT	METRIC	TYPE I	TYPE II	TYPE III	TYPE IV	OTHER
Personnel	Incident Commander (ICT1-5)	Yes	Yes	Yes	Yes	Yes
Personnel	Safety Officer (SOF1-3)	Yes	Yes	Yes		
Personnel	Information Officer (IOF1-3)	Yes	Yes	Yes		
Personnel	Operations Section Chief (OSC1-2)	2 ea.	2 ea.			
Personnel	Division/Group Supervisor	4 ea.				
Personnel	Air Operations Branch Director (AOBD)	Yes				
Personnel	Air Support Group Supervisor (ASG)	Yes				
Personnel	Air Tactical Group Supervisor (ATG)	Yes				
Personnel	Planning Section Chief (PSC 1-2)	Yes	Yes			
Personnel	Situation Unit Leader (SITL)	Yes				

RESOURCE: Incident Management Team, Firefighting

CATEGORY: Firefighting (ESF #4) | **KIND:** Team

MINIMUM CAPABILITIES:						
COMPONENT	METRIC	TYPE I	TYPE II	TYPE III	TYPE IV	OTHER
Personnel	Resource Unit Leader (RESL)	2 ea.				
Personnel	Fire Behavior Analyst (FBAN)	Yes				
Personnel	Logistics Section Chief (LSC 1-2)	Yes	Yes			
Personnel	Communications Unit Leader (COML)	Yes				
Personnel	Supply Unit Leader (SPUL)	Yes				
Personnel	Facilities Unit Leader (FACL)	Yes				
Personnel	Ground Support Unit Leader (GSUL)	Yes				
Personnel	Finance/Admin Section Chief (FSC 1-2)	Yes	Yes			
Personnel	Time Unit Leader (TIME)	Yes				
Personnel	Comp/Claims Unit Leader (COMP)	Yes				
Personnel	Procurement Unit Leader (PROC)	Yes				

FEMA 508-4 Typed Resource Definitions - Fire and Hazardous Materials Resources
07/20/2005

RESOURCE:	Incident Management Team, Firefighting				
CATEGORY:	Firefighting (ESF #4)			**KIND:**	Team
MINIMUM CAPABILITIES:	**TYPE I**	**TYPE II**	**TYPE III**	**TYPE IV**	**OTHER**
COMPONENT	**METRIC**				
COMMENTS:	Type I Incident Management Team				
	To become eligible for participating on a National Type I team, any person filling a team position as the Incident Commander, Safety Officer, Information Officer, or general staff must complete the Advanced Incident Management (S-520) training course.				
	Type II Incident Management Team				
	To become eligible for participation on a Type II team, any person filling a team position as the Incident Commander, Safety Officer, Information Officer, or general staff must complete the Command and General Staff (S-420) training course.				
	Type I Positions				
	Incident Commander Type I: Prerequisite experience includes satisfactory performance as an Incident Commander Type II; satisfactory position performance as an Incident Commander Type I on a wildland fire incident. Required Training: Advanced Incident Management (S-520).				
	Type II Positions				
	Incident Commander Type II: Prerequisite experience includes satisfactory performance as an Incident Commander Type III; satisfactory performance as an Operations Section Chief Type II; satisfactory position performance as an Incident Commander Type II on a wildland fire incident. Required Training: Command and General Staff (S-420). Additional Training: Advanced ICS (I-400), Incident Commander (S-400), Advanced Management Concepts (S-481).				
	Type III Positions				
	Incident Commander Type III: Prerequisite experience includes satisfactory performance as an Incident Commander Type IV; satisfactory performance as a Task Force Leader; satisfactory position performance as an Incident Commander Type III on a wildland fire incident. Required Training: Introduction to Wildland Fire Behavior Calculations (S-390). Additional Training: Incident Commander Extended Attack (S-300).				
	Type IV Positions				
	Incident Commander Type IV: Prerequisite experience includes satisfactory performance as a Single Resource Boss (Crew, Dozer, Engine, Tractor/Plow); satisfactory position performance as an Incident Commander Type IV on a wildland fire incident. Required Training: Fire Operations in the Urban Interface (S-215). Additional Training: Initial Attack Incident Commander (S-200), and Ignition Operations (S-234).				
	Type V Positions				
	Incident Commander Type V: Prerequisite experience includes satisfactory performance as an Advanced Firefighter/Squad Boss; satisfactory position performance as an Incident Commander Type V on a wildland fire incident. Required Training: Look Up, Look Down, Look Around (S-133). Additional Training: Intermediate Wildland Fire Behavior (S-290).				
	Source: National Wildfire Coordination Group (NWCG) Publication, National Interagency Incident Management System, Wildland and Prescribed Fire Qualifications System Guide, January 2000 (PMS 310-1, NFES 1414).				

RESOURCE: Interagency Buying Team, Firefighting

CATEGORY: Firefighting (ESF #4), Resource Management (ESF #7) **KIND:** Team

MINIMUM CAPABILITIES:

COMPONENT	METRIC	TYPE I	TYPE II	TYPE III	TYPE IV	OTHER
Personnel		6-member team consisting of a team leader, 4 members and 1 trainee position (used as needed) Personnel from the incident agency or alternate buying team members may be added, as needed, to supplement the primary team				
Personnel	Training (Recommended)	• I-200, Basic Incident Command System (12 classroom hours) • S-260, Incident Command Business Management (self-study) • D-110, Dispatch Recorder (16 classroom hours) • J-252, Ordering Manager • J-253, Receiving and Distribution • National Interagency Buying Team Guide (self-study) or Workshop • On-the-Job Training • Purchased Card and Convenience Check training • Procurement Unit Leader Training (S-360 Unit Leader)				

U.S. Department of Homeland Security
Federal Emergency Management Agency

Interagency Buying Team, Firefighting

RESOURCE:					
CATEGORY:	Firefighting (ESF #4), Resource Management (ESF #7)		**KIND:** Team		
MINIMUM CAPABILITIES:					
COMPONENT	**METRIC**	**TYPE I**	**TYPE II**	**TYPE III**	**TYPE IV**	**OTHER**
Equipment	Buying Team Kit	• Reference Material (see comments) • Internet/Intranet Web site References (see comments) • Supplies (see comments) • Forms (see comments) • Sample of Log Sheets (see comments)				

COMMENTS:

The Buying Team works through the local administrative staff to support procurement activities. Therefore, Buying Teams should be sensitive to and strive to operate within local policies and procedures. The members of the Buying Teams follow:

- The Buying Team Leader (BUYL) (1)

- The Assistant or Deputy Buying Team Leader (BUYL-D) (1)

- Buying Team Members (BUYM) (4)

General Roles of the Buying Team include the following:

- Support incident procurement through the administrative staff.

- Transition with the incident agency upon arrival. This includes obtaining status of all resource orders completed and outstanding to date, as well as initiating procedures for the handling of new orders by the Buying Team.

- Fill resource orders for services, supplies, and equipment from established sources (NFES Caches, GSA) and the open market and, for those which are not filled, by the dispatch community or the administrative unit's procurement activity. Reviews resource orders for completeness.

- Check on estimated times of departure and estimated times of arrival for pending resource orders.

- Obtain approval from the administrative staff or the IBA before purchasing any sensitive or questionable property.

- Provide the incident base (Finance Section Chief, Procurement Unit Leader, Logistics Section Chief, and Ground Support Unit Leader) an updated equipment log.

- Establish and maintain good working relationships and lines of communication.

- Update the incident service and supply plan with new sources and other information.

Buying Team Kit: Each Buying Team should have a kit containing the following items to take along when dispatched to an incident:

Reference Materials

RESOURCE:	Interagency Buying Team, Firefighting			
CATEGORY:	Firefighting (ESF #4), Resource Management (ESF #7)		KIND:	Team
MINIMUM CAPABILITIES:				
COMPONENT	METRIC	TYPE I	TYPE II	TYPE III	TYPE IV	OTHER

METRIC (TYPE I):

- Interagency Incident Business Management Handbook, NWCG Handbook 2, NFES 1139
- National Interagency Mobilization Guide, NFES 2091 (NFES 2092 for half-size)
- Activity Calendar (Optional Form 67 or similar)
- NWCG National Fire Equipment System Catalog, Part I, Fire Supplies & Equipment (NFES 0362, Part I & Part II when using order #0362)
- NWCG National Fire Equipment System Catalog, Part II Publications (NFES 3362)

Internet/Intranet Web site References

- NWCG Internet homepage: http://www.nwcg.gov
- Forest Service Fire & Aviation Internet homepage: http://www.fs.fed.us/fire/
- Forest Service Acquisition Management Intranet homepage: http://fsweb.wo.fs.fed.us/aqm/
- BLM Intranet: http://webtst.nifc.blm.gov/Sascher/blmintranet/Index.htm
- NIFC and related governmental agency links (BLM, BIA, FWS, NPS, NWS): http://www.nifc.gov

Supplies

- Battery powered or solar powered handheld calculator
- Spare batteries
- Highlighters
- Stapler and staple remover
- Other supplies as needed
- (Optional) First Aid kit and a bloodborne pathogens barrier kit

Forms, See exhibits to the National Interagency Buying Team Guide and the Interagency Incident Business Management Handbook for sample forms.

Sample of Log Sheets

- Resource Order Log (Leader and Deputy Only)
- Purchase Card Log Sheets
- Convenience Check Log Sheets

Source: National Wildfire Coordinating Group (NWCG) Publication, National Interagency Buying Team Guide, December 1999 (PMS 315).

RESOURCE:	Mobile Communications Unit (Law/Fire)			
CATEGORY:	Communications		KIND: Vehicle	
MINIMUM CAPABILITIES:				
COMPONENT	METRIC	TYPE I	TYPE II	TYPE III	TYPE IV	OTHER

COMPONENT	METRIC	TYPE I	TYPE II	TYPE III	TYPE IV	OTHER
Equipment	Console/ Workstation	2	2			
Equipment	Frequency Cap.	Multi Range	Multi Range			
Equipment	Power Source	Internal	Internal			
Equipment	Telephone System	6 Trunk/16 Extensions				
Personnel	Personnel	2	2			
COMMENTS:	Multi Range: 150-174 MHz, 450-470 MHz, 800 MHz (Simplex or Repeated), Single Range: 150-174 MHz only					

FEMA 508-4 Typed Resource Definitions - Fire and Hazardous Materials Resources
07/20/2005

FEMA

Portable Pump

RESOURCE:		Portable Pump			
CATEGORY:	Firefighting		KIND:	Equipment	
MINIMUM CAPABILITIES:					
COMPONENT	METRIC	TYPE I	TYPE II	TYPE III	TYPE IV	OTHER
Equipment	Pumping Capacity (GPM)	500	250	50		
COMMENTS:	These are normally trailer mounted units.				

RESOURCE:	Strike Team, Engine (Fire)				
CATEGORY:	Firefighting (ESF #4); Search & Rescue (ESF #9)			KIND:	Team
MINIMUM CAPABILITIES:		TYPE I	TYPE II	TYPE III	TYPE IV	OTHER
COMPONENT	METRIC	TYPE I	TYPE II	TYPE III	TYPE IV	OTHER
Equipment	Engine, Fire	5	5	5	5	(See Engine for details)
Personnel	STL	1	1	1	1	Strike Team Task Force Leader
Personnel	Engine	4	3	3	3	Staffing on each Engine
Personnel	Total	21	16	16	16	
COMMENTS:	Strike Team defined as like number of resources, with common communications, and a leader. Engine Strike Team Typing is based on individual Engine Typing.					

RESOURCE:

CATEGORY:	Hazardous Materials Response (ESF #10)		KIND:	Team	

U.S. Coast Guard National Strike Force

MINIMUM CAPABILITIES:

COMPONENT See Note 1	METRIC	TYPE I	TYPE II	TYPE III	TYPE IV	OTHER
Equipment	Chemical Release					Chemical Response Trailers; Level A, B, and C PPE suits
Equipment	Air, Liquids, and Solids					• Flame and Photo Ionization Detectors • Fluorometers • Particulate Meters • Soil and Sludge Sample Kits • pH meters • Decontamination Equipment • Portable Weather stations • Drum lifters • EMT kits • Chlorine kits
Equipment	Small Boats					• 32-foot and 24-foot Munsons • 15-foot Inflatable boats • 18-foot John boats
Equipment	Lighting/ Pumping Equipment					• Ready Pump Loads • High-capacity, hydraulically driven, centrifugal submersible pumps capable of transferring oil and

RESOURCE:						
U.S. Coast Guard National Strike Force						
CATEGORY:	Hazardous Materials Response (ESF #10)		KIND:	Team		
MINIMUM CAPABILITIES:						
COMPONENT See Note 1	METRIC	TYPE I	TYPE II	TYPE III	TYPE IV	OTHER
						• chemicals or dewatering • Nonsubmersible diaphragm and peristaltic pumps capable of transferring oil and chemicals (medium/small capacity) • Hydraulic prime movers and support equipment
Equipment	Communications Equipment					Communications support equipment ranges from handheld radios to portable satellite communications repeater systems
Equipment	Oil Discharges					• Vessel of Opportunity Skimming System (VOSS) • Inflatable (45-inch) boom (6,000 feet) • Temporary Storage Devices
Equipment	Damage Control and Support					• Oil/water interface meter • Plugging and patching equipment • Generators (3.0 KW to 10 KW)
Equipment	Special Monitoring Equipment					• Radiological detection capabilities • Dispersant operations

RESOURCE:	U.S. Coast Guard National Strike Force				
CATEGORY:	Hazardous Materials Response (ESF #10)		**KIND:**	Team	
MINIMUM CAPABILITIES:					
COMPONENT See Note 1	**METRIC**	**TYPE I**	**TYPE II**	**TYPE III**	**TYPE IV**	**OTHER**
Equipment	Photographic Equipment					• 35 mm and digital cameras • Video cameras and players
Equipment	Vehicle Command Post					• Tractor/trailer units • Mobile Incident Command Posts • All-terrain vehicles

COMMENTS: **Note 1:** NSF Specialized Response Equipment

There are only three National Strike Force teams in the Nation. All three National Strike Force teams have the same level of capability, which exceeds the standards set in the Mutual Aid definition of a Type I Hazardous Materials Entry Team. However, because of their deployment capabilities and versatility, they are simply classified as "Other." The U.S. Coast Guard National Strike Force (NSF) was created in 1973 as a Coast Guard special force under the National Contingency Plan (NCP/see 40 CFR 300.145) to respond to oil and hazardous chemical incidents. The National Strike Force is comprised of three 40-member Strike Teams and the National Strike Force Coordination Center (NSFCC), which manages, supports, and set standards for the three teams. The three teams are: the Atlantic Strike Team in Fort Dix, NJ; the Gulf Strike Team in Mobile, AL; and the Pacific Strike Team in Novato, CA.

The NSF is recognized worldwide as an expert in preparedness and response to mitigate the effects of oil discharges and hazardous substance releases. Its mandate is to assist and support USCG and EPA Federal On-Scene Coordinators (FOSCs) with their response and preparedness activities to protect the public health and welfare and the environment. Although its three primary missions are pollution response, training, and planning, the NSFCC also houses a Public Information Assist Team (PIAT), which is capable of providing public affairs support as well as crisis communication and Joint Information Center (JIC) expertise to FOSCs during a response.

NSF Qualification Program:

The NSF Qualification Program includes four levels. Although these levels are unique to the NSF, our personnel meet training and skill requirements similar to those established in 29 CFR 1910.120 (g) (6).

• Response Member (RM): Is trained in more than 50 areas of oil and HazMat response operations and attains an awareness level of all NSF Equipment. This allows the RM to perform a number of vital functions in a pollution response, primarily assisting the RT.

• Response Technician (RT): Is a significant level beyond the RM and is the position reached by most Strike Team members. An RT is qualified to operate all NSF equipment. An RT has also attended pollution response specialist courses and obtained significant field experience on oil and HazMat incidents.

• Response Supervisor (RS): Is a level beyond RT and supervises the technical aspects of NSF response operations at oil or HazMat incidents. This includes the preparation, deployment, and operation of all NSF equipment. The RS helps a response in many areas, including directing operations, response planning, resolving site safety issues, and solving technical problems.

FEMA

RESOURCE:	U.S. Coast Guard National Strike Force			
CATEGORY:	Hazardous Materials Response (ESF #10)		KIND:	Team
MINIMUM CAPABILITIES:				
COMPONENT	METRIC			
See Note 1	TYPE I	TYPE II	TYPE III	TYPE IV	OTHER

- Response Officer (RO): Is a senior leadership position filled by a commissioned or warrant officer. An RO manages all aspects of any size NSF response, including response planning, mobilization, and operations. An RO receives significant resident and unit training, and field experience. An RO can fill key positions in a spill management team, direct operations, liaise with senior officials, resolve safety issues, recommend alternative countermeasures, explain policies, and solve crisis management problems.

Water Tender, Firefighting (Tanker)

RESOURCE:					
CATEGORY:	Firefighting (ESF #4)			**KIND:**	Equipment
MINIMUM CAPABILITIES:		**TYPE I**	**TYPE II**	**TYPE III**	**TYPE IV**	**OTHER**
COMPONENT	**METRIC**					
Equipment	2,000 gallon	2,000 gallon	1,000 gallon	1,000 gallon	2,000 gallon	
Equipment	300 GPM	300 GPM	120 GPM	50 GPM	300 GPM	
COMMENTS:						

www.ingramcontent.com/pod-product-compliance
Lightning Source LLC
Chambersburg PA
CBHW080748290526

45790CB00008B/3373